CHOSEN FOR CONFLICT

LEADING IN OPPOSITION

BRIAN DUPOR

CONTENTS

A WORD FROM THE AUTHOR

I believe godly leadership is essential in these evil and dangerous times. There is a call for godly leaders to arise to accomplish the work that God is doing in these last days. We are witnessing intense conflict and opposition against the kingdom of heaven. Nevertheless, God has given us strategies to lead through these adverse times. I am a son of God, a devoted husband to my lovely wife, and I'm blessed to have her labor beside me. I'm a teacher, mentor, and leader. God has appointed me to train up our two sons, whom God has called to be leaders in their generation. Also, I have been entrusted with a ministry called We Are One Kingdom Ministries. This move of God started during a time of oppression, hopelessness, and corruption within that community. God had charged me with leading men to a place of freedom in Christ, authentic worship, godly character, unity, and service to others. I could not accomplish this assignment on my own. I was aided by other great men of God who had a mind to work. Men who had a checkered past like me but who have also been transformed by the power of Jesus Christ. Through our transformation in Christ, we were able to influence the culture around us and usher in true revival. I know firsthand the spiritual opposition that leaders face. Not all leaders are effective in leading during full-out spiritual relentless assaults. Intense conflict can be confusing, frustrating, and tiresome. Many leaders are in a place where they do not know how to start, continue, rebuild, or finish the work that God has given them, which leaves the leader feeling defeated.

For this reason, I am grateful that these words have found themselves in your possession. These writings are to equip, educate, encourage, and empower the leader. You have taken on a brave and noble task.

Whether you lead a household, a church, or a business. If you are a leader within the community, nationally or globally, I must thank you for standing up to the call and saying yes to that cause. I know what a yes to God requires. One must count the cost of following Christ and leading His people. A yes is an unwavering commitment and sacrifice. A "yes" is a declaration that you have decided to serve God and God alone. A "yes" is accepting that the world will hate and reject you. A "yes" is a bold state of surrender and willingness to suffer for the sake of Christ.

I hope to impart wisdom to give you the right perspective to act. We will focus on twelve principles as we journey through this book. These writings present biblical illustrations and scriptural references associated with the twelve principles imparted to you. Following each principle are introspection moments that could also serve as discussion questions for small groups. These introspection moments were designed to aid you in evaluating yourself and the people you are called to lead. Together, we will uncover the conflicts launched by our enemy to hinder and discourage the work of God. We will expose the conflicts within ourselves as leaders and how to navigate them. I am authoring this book for those who are leading even when there is doubt within yourselves. I know it is challenging, dark, and lonely; however, if you are a real leader, you cannot quit or turn back even though quitting seems easier.

The vision that God has given me is for this book to be an easy-to-read reference tool you can pick up whenever you need to while in the middle of the battle. May our great God cause you to triumph through Jesus Christ and finish strong.

INTRODUCTION

"For the earnest expectation of the creature waiteth for the manifestation of the sons of God"
(ROMANS 8:19 KJV)

Many people wonder if this is the end of the world as we know it. No, this is not the end just yet. We are in a time of mercy and longsuffering. Through pride, stubbornness, and arrogance, we have rejected God and witnessed our destruction befalling us. However, God is not to blame. Let us not make the mistake of vindicating ourselves while accusing God. What is required in this hour is the sacrifice of godly sorrow and repentance. May we humbly acknowledge our wrongs against God and each other. Only by humbling ourselves and quickly turning from our corrupt and wicked ways can we ever experience healing and true restoration.

In our respective nations, we have witnessed a great imbalance in the economy, government, health, education, and religious systems. Our homes, businesses, churches, and communities have all been impacted in ways we never imagined. Make no mistake: in the absence of godly leadership, there is corruption, confusion, division, and evil works. If you allow corruption to remain, then destruction is inevitable. Nations, communities, families, and churches desperately need God's chosen leaders who possess divine strategies and solutions. The rebuilding process will occur, but it must first begin within us.

This assignment will take more than sheer willpower or self-help books. We need more than great intellectual knowledge and motivational speeches to rebuild what was destroyed. It will take more than just counseling sessions or stimulus packages to help our families through these challenging times. Rehabilitation programs within prison institutions are great. However, only the power of God can bring about transformation in the hearts of those behind the walls. In times past, we may have made it through our titles, status, or associations. However, in these times, those things will not bring success in God. Your success will only come through an authentic relationship with the Creator and obedience to His Word. We cannot replace or avoid Him any longer. It is God Almighty who will empower you for this task. You cannot do this on your strength. Egos will have to be checked at the door. Only those who walk in the fear of God will persevere and do great work in these last days. God is raising leaders from His own heart. Leaders whom he has called out, confronted, and changed by His great power. Our great God has poured out His spirit and has pricked your heart to follow His purpose for your life.

Many of you are not content with where you are or the conditions around you. You crave more, and you desire true change. Good, because I believe God has called you to raise a standard. It is time to restore the walls of justice and execute righteousness throughout our nations. You may feel inadequate or unqualified. Keep in mind feelings change, but they do not make change. You must know and believe that God has chosen you for such an appointed time as this. You were chosen for conflict, so do not be fearful or timid; God is with you. Leading comes with great opposition, and it will take our great God to accomplish what seems impossible. I pray that God will lead you through the opposition and conflicts you are experiencing. As the Lord leads you, may you lead others into a place of freedom, peace, prosperity, and wholeness that can only be found in Jesus Christ. The twelve principles in this book will give you clarity and direction and empower you to lead fearlessly. May we begin.

01

MADE IN HIS IMAGE

"So God created man in his own image, in the image of God created he him; male and female created he them"

(GENESIS 1:27 KJV)

In today's culture, image is everything. The image is our billboard to the world around us. It is our unique expression to others. That is why we go to great lengths to protect our image. After all, no one wants to be misrepresented. We spend countless hours on social media updating our profiles and editing the perfect snapshot. Millions of dollars are spent by corporations on marketing and advertisement to draw customers to their brands. We want the world to know who we are and what we are about. Let us examine that word image. Image simply means visible representation. In the beginning, when God created man, He created him in His image. He made Adam His visible representation on earth. To represent someone means you have the authority to act and speak on that person's behalf. God had given Adam the authority to act and speak on behalf of God in the earth. Adam wasn't God, but God had delegated a level of authority to him. Not only did God create man in His image, but He also created man in His likeness. Likeness speaks to the resemblance and quality of something or someone. In Luke 6:36KJV, the Bible says, "Be ye therefore merciful, as your Father also is merciful." We resemble our Father in heaven when we show mercy. Leviticus 19:2 says, "Speak unto all the congregation of the children of Israel, and say unto them, Ye shall be holy: for I, the Lord your God, am holy." When we walk in holiness, we resemble our Father in heaven.

Reflect on the times you were told that you resemble your earthly mother or father. Usually, it would be how you smile or your need to keep things organized like your parents. Why would others say that you resemble your parents? Because they see in you a quality that reminds them of the source from which you come. In today's culture, God's chosen leaders must learn to bear God's image and likeness. In every action you take as a leader, through every word you speak or direction you give, do so as God's image bearer. Filter every word and decision through the leading of God's spirit and word. Ask yourself if God would approve of this course of action. You must act and speak knowing that you represent God. We are ambassadors of Jesus Christ, meaning we represent the agenda of the Kingdom of Heaven. You cannot afford to lead others in your flesh and to serve your agenda. God is spirit, and His true sons are those who are led by His spirit. What are the characteristics of God's spirit that we must carry?

Galatians 5:22-23 KJV says, "But the fruit of the Spirit is love, joy, peace, longsuffering, gentleness, goodness, faith, meekness, temperance; against such there is no law." Nothing worse than being under a hateful, joyless, impatient, rigid, wicked, faithless, prideful, arrogant, and undisciplined leader. The only way to be a spirit-filled leader who resembles the Father is to remain connected to the source (God). The more time you spend with a person, the more you begin to imitate their ways. Spend time with the Father in His word and learn from Him. Practice His commands that He teaches us in His Holy scriptures. Let His statutes be your guide for living, leading, and loving well.

"And God blessed them, and God said unto them, Be fruitful, and multiply, and replenish the earth, and subdue it: and have dominion over the fish of the sea, and over the fowl of the air, and over every living thing that moveth upon the earth"

(GENESIS 1:28 KJV)

God commanded Adam to be fruitful. To be fruitful means to be made up of, consistent with procreation, or to be able to reproduce. Being fruitful speaks to producing new individuals of the same kind and causing them to exist again. God was telling Adam that the same image and likeness in which I made you, I want you to reproduce the same kind and multiply it. Do not change the quality of it. I want you to carry it on. In John 15:8, KJV says, "Herein is my Father glorified, that ye bear much fruit; so, shall ye be my disciples." Jesus was teaching His disciples that they could not be fruitful alone. The only way to bear fruit was to remain in the Vine. Jesus is the vine, so if we remain in Christ and Christ remains in us, we will be able to bear fruit, for we cannot do anything apart from God.

As a leader, you must understand this principle. The principle of how to remain. We are nothing without God, so we must stay in fellowship and connection with our Source. Do not allow anything or anyone to separate you from your life source. Do not allow people or the pressures of life to distract and withdraw you from your Creator. I always tell people that the husband that my wife fell in love with is the man who is clinging to Christ. The moment I disconnect from my source or put her above my source is the moment I no longer resemble the man she fell in love with. The man I am apart from Christ is selfish, inconsiderate, impatient, insecure, unfaithful, indecisive, and impulsive. The father my sons need to raise them is the man who abides in Christ. If I do not practice remaining, I cannot give my sons a true model to imitate.

Children are looking for a source to identify with and to imitate. Why do you think so many of our young men and women are joining gangs? Many are immersing themselves in the worldly culture around them. They are attracted to the wrong images that they see. These false images are advertised, marketed, and presented to our youth. The father and source of these false images is Satan himself. The father of all lies is captivating and deceiving our youth by promising them the kingdoms of the world. He promises them money, acceptance by the world, power, and pleasure. In exchange, he temps and seduces our youth to worship him instead of the one true God. Our children are captivated and conforming to these false images that lead them to destruction. As fathers and mothers, we must intervene. Let us model Christlike behavior so our children can have a reference to respect and imitate. You bear that responsibility as a father, mother, and leader, so you cannot afford to disconnect or stay distant from Jesus Christ. Never allow anyone, not even your family, to pull you away from remaining in Christ. Do not make the mistake of putting your career, family, or possessions above God. The moment you reduce God in your value system, you reduce yourself to self-destruction. The image of God in you becomes distorted, and you no longer reflect His glory in your life to others around you. Our identity is in Christ and not in this world. God is conforming you back into His image, which is the image of Christ.

> **The moment you reduce God in your value system, you reduce yourself to self-destruction**

We must tear down this worldly image of ourselves in exchange for the glorious image of Jesus Christ. It was always God's desire for His image bearers to reflect the same qualities as Him. We are called to resemble His character and authority while on earth. Hence, this is why God told Adam to multiply. God's purpose was to have Adam produce more children who would bear His image and likeness. Their children were to multiply while bearing God's image and likeness. He desired for a righteous seed to exist on the earth perpetually. Now, it makes sense when God tells Adam to replenish the earth. The word replenish means to fill. The reason God wanted the earth to be replenished was because God wanted the earth to be filled with His image and glory.

Now God says once you fill the earth, Adam, I want you to subdue it. The word subdue means to conquer and bring under control. Subdue also means to prevent something from existing or developing. God wanted Adam to be His agent on earth and prevent some things from developing and existing. I told you that you were created and chosen for conflict. Many things around us are not in order, which is wrong. God is calling for His image bearers to subdue. To prevent and stop these unrighteous acts from developing and occurring. Yes, we are called to prevent and stop the enemies' plans in our homes, communities, and nations. Everywhere that God plants you, He leads you to subdue that area for the kingdom of heaven and to reveal His glory in that region. Once you learn to subdue as you walk in God's authority and display His spirit, you can take dominion.

As a leader, you cannot have dominion over something that you have not brought into subjection to God. It is all or nothing. It starts with our heart, mind, and strength. If you want God to have dominion and rule within you, submit yourselves as a living sacrifice so that the life of Christ may be revealed in you. God can fill a heart that is submitted with the capacity to love unconditionally. God can renew and transform a mind that is submitted into the mind of Christ. We need the mind of Christ so we can have the correct perspective in our daily lives. When you have God's perspective on a matter, then it shapes your attitude and behavior. Which leads you to take godly action and bring about godly results. Once you are in submission and governed by God, everything around you can begin to align.

You must be the first partaker and surrender to God. Confront the battles within before you set out to the battle withal you. This goes for the battle for your household, community, and church. Husbands, you must submit to Christ if you expect your wife and children to submit to you. Also, wives must learn to submit to Christ and their husbands so their children may learn. They will learn obedience and submission as they watch their parents model this virtue within the home and in their relationship with God. If there is no evidence of fruit within you, do not expect things to be fruitful around you. As a leader, you must continuously grow and increase in the fruit of God's spirit to cause growth and increase around you. Yes, we need to replenish and fill our area of dominion with God's glory. Where there is no strength in numbers, bringing assigned territories under subjection and preventing wickedness from developing will be difficult. You need those who are one in spirit, mind, and purpose within the kingdom to join forces, which is why the gospel of Jesus Christ is so important. The power of the gospel of Jesus Christ is strong enough to win the souls of men over.

If there is no evidence of fruit within you, do not expect things to be fruitful around you.

The Kingdom church is so important in this hour. It is time we stopped competing against one another and started forming cohesiveness. Until we do, we will not experience true dominion in our areas of influence. Dominion means to govern by exercising rule, leadership, and oversight. Dominion also speaks to controlling the actions, affairs, and implementing policies within a specific territory. We need each other as the body of Christ to reveal the wisdom of God to the world around us. Together, we could influence the diversities of affairs while implementing godly policies and principles. Once this is accomplished, we will see the kingdom of heaven gain ground in our schools, communities, and land.

THE GREAT EXCHANGE

"And the woman said unto the serpent, We may eat of the fruit of the trees of the garden: But of the fruit of the tree which is in the midst of the garden, God hath said, Ye shall not eat of it, neither shall ye touch it, lest ye die. And the serpent said unto the woman, Ye shall not surely die"

(GENESIS 3:2-4 KJV)

One of the main causes of the fall of man is because the first man, Adam, neglected to subdue. He allowed the enemy to invade his territory, and he failed to obey the truth and commands of God. Before this great tragedy, Adam was operating in the wisdom of God, knowledge of God, and understanding of God. Adam had the image of God, the likeness of God, and the blessing of God. He was lacking nothing. God had given everything freely to Adam except for the tree of the knowledge of good and evil. There was no good thing that God withheld from Adam. The biggest deception of the enemy is to make you believe that God is withholding something good from you. The trouble comes when we attempt to determine what is good for our lives without a transformed mind. Unless you have had your mind renewed by God, then you will not have the ability to prove God's acceptable will. Remember, God knows how to give good gifts to His children. Every good and perfect gift comes from God. There is no good thing apart from God. Many people want to know why God would allow the tree of good and evil to be placed in the garden in the first place. I always tell people if others only love you when you tell them yes and do not love you the same when you tell them no, then that indicates that it was never love in the first place. That is why God said in

John 14:21 KJV, "He that hath my commandments, and keepeth them, it is he that loveth me: and he that loveth me shall be loved of my Father, and I will love him, and will manifest myself to him." If God never respected your no to Him and only gave you the option to say yes, then it is not love; it is an abuse of power and control. Similarly, God gives each person the option to say yes to Him or to say no and reject Him. Those who are not fully persuaded that God is love, that God is good, and that He will never withhold any good thing from them will never fully trust Him. Refusing to submit and obey God, we yield our will to the enemy. That is exactly what Adam did on that dreadful day. He did not submit to God in obedience and yielded his will to Satan. Since that tragic day, man has been in a stubborn state of rebellion, refusing to turn back to God in repentance.

LEADERSHIP PRINCIPLE 1:
Live and Lead in the Image of Christ

Every person born after Adam came into the world without God's image but was born into the image of Adam. The image of Adam represents being brought forth in a sinful state and body. We must choose Jesus Christ to be reborn again of spirit and conform to the image of Jesus Christ, who is the image of God. To walk in divine victory and dominion, we must bear His image. When speaking with his disciples, Jesus gave us a key point about Him being the way, the truth, and the life. Jesus explained that no one can come to the Father except by coming through the Son. If you know the Son, Jesus Christ, then you have known and seen the Father. The disciples wrestled with this idea and told Jesus to show them the Father. Jesus tells them I spent so much time with you, and you still do not know me. If you see me, you have seen the Father. In John 14:10 KJV, Jesus tells them, "Believest thou not that I am in the Father, and the Father in me? The words that I speak unto you I speak not of myself: but the Father that dwelleth in me, he doeth the works." If we are going to do the greater works, we must allow the spirit of God that resides inside us to operate. Those around us should be able to see a reflection of Jesus as you bear the image of Christ.

Scripture references to read:

- **John 14:5-12,**
- **Romans 5:12-19,**
- **Romans 8:29,**
- **1 Corinthians 15:21-22,**
- **Ephesians 2,**
- **Galatians 5:22-23,**
- **Genesis 1**

Introspection Moment

1) Who have I patterned my life after?
2) How would those connected to me describe my character?
3) What areas in my life that I confess are not under total submission to God?
4) What actionable step can I take today to prevent the enemy from distorting the image of Christ in my life?

Key Terms

Define the terms below in your own words.

A. Image-

B. Fruitful-

C. Multiply-

D. Replenish-

E. Subdue-

F. Dominion-

02

POSITIONED FOR PREPARATION

"For if thou remain completely silent at this time, relief and deliverance will arise for the Jews from another place, but you and your father's house will perish. Yet who knows whether you have come to the kingdom for such a time as this"

(ESTHER 4:14 NKJV)

Leadership is an invitation and a call from God. He is calling His children out of hiding and preparing them to reveal the light of His glory. His glory is meant to manifest in the earth where there is so much darkness. He has strategically prepared and positioned you to fulfill His good pleasure on the earth. However, God's preparation is not an event but a lifelong process. While in preparation for leadership, God will teach and refine you through the hardship and opposition you will encounter. The story of Esther is a testament to that very truth. The book of Esther takes place during a time when the Jews had been taken captive by a foreign nation called Babylon. They were carried away to live in a culture unlike their own and with people who did not serve the God of their fathers. However, there was a man named Mordecai who was one of the Jews taken captive. He adopted his niece Hadassah, also known as Esther, because her mother and father were both dead. Mordecai took Esther as his daughter and cared for her. Meanwhile, the King of Babylon had banished his former queen from the palace because she publicly dishonored him during the king's banquet. Therefore, the king desired to replace his former queen with someone honorable. Sometimes, God will use conflicts as an opportunity for you to be used as an instrument in His hands to bring change and solutions.

Nevertheless, the king decreed that all the young ladies who were virgins be gathered and brought into the palace. The women were to go through intense purifications and preparations. This was a necessary process because the young lady, at the end of the process, would be crowned Queen. As a young virgin, Esther was one of many selected to enter the palace. The king was pleased with Esther's beauty, and she obtained favor from the King. She was appointed the best place in the palace and the best spa treatments money could buy. Nevertheless, Mordecai, in his wisdom, instructed Esther not to tell any member of her family or any of her fellow Jews. When God chooses you and escorts you into high places, it is not always wise to share this news immediately. Not even with those of your household. Use divine discretion and wait until an appointed time. We will return to this point later. After the spa treatments and purifications ended. Esther was chosen out of all the women to be queen to the king. However, Mordecai admonished Esther not to get comfortable in her newfound position and forget about where she came from or her purpose. We can learn something from Mordecai, who warns the Queen. Let us not take the favor of God and fill ourselves with pride. Do not forget where we once were before He rescued us. You are not chosen to please yourself but for God's purpose and good pleasure. Queen Esther understood this and followed her uncle's advice. Promotion and leadership at this level do not come without opposition. While you celebrate your upward mobility, the enemy is busy conspiring for your downward spiral. The enemy used Haman's pride, jealousy, and ambition to conduct his work.

Haman, being a descendant of King Agag, who ruled the Amalekites, already had a deep disgust for the Jews. He is often called "the persecutor of the Jews" throughout the book of Esther. The Amalekites were known enemies of the Jews, and their origin was from Amalek, the grandson of Esau. Esau was the brother of Jacob, who was later named Israel. Esau and Jacob had a sibling rivalry with each other. Esau despised his birthright and sold it to his brother Jacob in exchange for food. Amalek came from this lineage of Esau, a people who despised their birthright. These people did not see the value in God and His promises. When God delivered the people of Israel out of Egypt and allowed them to pass between the Red Sea on dry land. The Amalekites were the first enemy that Israel encountered on the other side. We will discuss this further in a later chapter. Haman had just been promoted above other leaders and became the king's chief's elected official in his court. Haman was angry because Mordecai did not bow out of respect when he passed by him. From that moment, Haman took his anger not just out on Mordecai but was determined to destroy all the Jews.

Esther used her position of favor and honor to eventually deliver her people from the enemy who conspired to execute all the Jews. Despite Esther growing up as a slave in a foreign nation, disadvantaged because she was void of a mother and father. God positioned her and used her circumstances as preparation for her purpose. If God had not positioned Esther in the King's court, then the Jews would have been annihilated. What does this say about us? It does not matter where you were born or if you were adopted. Even if you have been labeled a felon and are facing incarceration right now. In the middle of your captivity, God has positioned you to prepare you to lead and do remarkable things for His glory. I challenge you to identify the conflicts around you. Pray about ways that God could use you to bring about change. Be available for the master's use. In His hands, your family can be saved. God can use you to help restore the community and city. Your nation could be redeemed because you were ordained with value and purpose to be used for God's glory. We are all Esther's born into slavery and living as strangers in a foreign land. However, God has chosen us and lavished us with His great love and favor. He caused goodness and mercy to pursue us all the days of our life. He has brought us into His kingdom of Righteousness through His son, Jesus Christ. Jesus sacrificed His life so we may have forgiveness of sins and inherit everlasting life. He has crowned us with deliverance and honor. Therefore, the enemy's conspiracy to destroy God's people will not prosper. I declare the word of God over your life; every weapon formed to destroy you will not succeed. This is not the end for you; the authority and power of Jesus Christ shall silence every lying tongue that has tried to revolt against you. I petition the favor of God to invade your life. May every setback, every hindering spirit, every assignment, plot, and scheme be dismantled. Turn it around, oh God, and cause this vessel to tread over snakes and scorpions as you have positioned them to do wonderful things by your spirit. May they come to know You and your son Jesus Christ whom you sent. With your grace and truth, may they lead courageously in opposition; amen.

Many are eager to take on the mantle of leadership but have not been a student of hardship. Not that you have not experienced hardship, but that you never allow the hardship to develop experience within you. God wants to develop you while you are on the battlefield. He wants to train your hands to war. Through these lessons, you will gain divine perspectives and strategies to navigate through conflict effectively. You will be equipped to train the people you are leading in the godly principles written in this book. You will be able to discern and identify various forms of opposition you encounter. Also, you will know how to stand courageously and strategically as a godly leader. After reading this book, your mind will be prepared for spiritual opposition. You will have a fresh perspective and attitude about the conflicts you face daily.

How will you lead others through challenging times if you never gain the fruit of patience that is reaped through suffering? Be diligent in pursuing God as He prepares you for this magnificent work. Through your opposition, God will confront and reveal the truth to you. This is where truth in the Holy scriptures challenges you, and grace empowers you. Conflicts within yourself will begin to arise. Opposition and trials have a way of revealing and refining what is really on the inside of us. God's word has a way of doing this as well. I recommend reading this book and having a Bible next to you. When intently searched, the Bible tends to serve as a mirror to show us our motives and what is in our hearts. The Word of God also shows us God's will and His heart towards us. While searching the Holy scriptures, you will get a glimpse of the mystery of Christ, who is the truth. This is when lies wrongly believed concerning our lives are confronted and expelled. As you choose to consistently believe and walk in the truth of God, you will experience a freedom that knows no bounds. Guilt and shame will turn into repentance and freedom. John 1:12 KJV says, "But as many as received Him, to them gave the power to become the sons of God, even to them that believe on His name." God has crowned you with glory, not limitations and shame. Do not let the enemy or man place limitations and guilt on your head where your crown sits. Allow the word of God to feed your faith, and let the trials ordained by God exercise your faith. May you be found fit for the master's use.

In addition, be patient in the process. Your perspective of God and your approach to God will radically change if you are patient and submissive through the process. For in the process, He gives you glimpses of His glory, revealing His power, nature, and heart to you. The residue of insecurities, bitterness, and anger will come to the surface. Do not worry or quit. These are just signs that healing and deliverance are taking place. All doubt, jealousy, selfish ambition, and greed will be brought to the forefront. Any denial, offenses, and damaged layers of your soul will manifest and be confronted with the truth of God. In this place of vulnerability, you gain a godly fear of who God is. You will be broken and humbled before the Lord. However, you will receive a revelation of God's love for you and be sustained by His grace. Remain submissive to God during this process of preparation. After you are broken, God will rebuild you into an authentically strong and godly leader.

LEADERSHIP PRINCIPLE 2:
Accept and Receive Sonship

Before accepting the call to leadership, you must first acknowledge and receive God's call to sonship. Sonship refers to the relationship a child has with his father. As a child of God, you partake of the divine nature by virtue of God's power. You bear His image and likeness in all that you do. A son imitates what he watches his father do. A son also holds the rights to his father's inheritance. This is where you move from the mindset and spirit of a slave. Into the mind and spirit of Jesus Christ, who is the son of God. Without sonship, you will always function and operate like a slave; having no authentic identity, no authority, no freedom, no privileges, no kingdom influence, and no legitimate strength to lead.

Scripture references to read:

- **Galatians 4:4-6,**
- **John 1:12-13,**
- **John 3:5-6,**
- **2 Peter 1: 4,**
- **2 Corinthians 6:17-18.**

Introspection Moment

1) Do I find it hard to view God as a Father in my life? If so, then why?
2) What is the difference between a son and a slave mindset?
3) Which mindset do I currently possess and why?
4) What actionable steps must I take to build a better relationship with my Father in Heaven?

KNOW THE STATE
OF THE PEOPLE

"And they said unto me, the remnant that are left of the captivity there in the province are in great affliction and reproach: the wall of Jerusalem also is broken down, and the gates there of are burned with fire"

(NEHEMIAH 1:3 KJV)

Unfortunately, too many leaders are blinded and consumed by their vision, position, and results. We can become insensitive to those around us and those who help us achieve our goals. One of the biggest lessons that the Lord taught me is to know the state of the people. Do not be so performance-driven that you disregard what drives the people behind the work. You must lead those you are called to lead with compassion for. This compassion will not only be the attribute that sets you apart as a great and effective leader. Also, it will serve as the fuel you need to lead with precision and passion through tough times. Nehemiah understood this principle. Nehemiah served as an official cupbearer under King Artaxerxes' administration and was a trusted advisor to the king. This office was very influential, which afforded Nehemiah the favor of the King. Although Nehemiah had this prominent office; still, he had a heart for his people who were not as fortunate. He asked about his people's state and discovered they were suffering and disgraced. He also discovered that the wall of Jerusalem had been broken down, and their gates were on fire. This was a tragedy for the people of Jerusalem. During that time, the wall of a city represented its strength and security. The wall kept the city safe from enemies seeking to take what was valuable from within the city. This means if a wall was destroyed, then the people were exposed and defenseless. Many people around us are in similar conditions. They are exposed to Satan's attacks, and they are without defense. You would be surprised to know the state of mind of people you may be living with, working with, or worshipping with. Many are defenseless and hopeless. Many are weighed down with anxiety, loneliness, depression, insecurities, and shame. Many leaders today fall into this category as well. You may even feel that this description fits you. Be encouraged; God is greater than any of these feelings. I speak the peace of God over your mind, emotions, houses, jobs, churches, and everything attached to you. To discern the state of the people, you must seek God's face on their behalf. Ask God to give you discernment and eyes to see the hearts of those around you. Ask for attentive ears to hear the concerns of the people. To know your people, you must be willing to observe and prioritize the time to listen. This applies even in our very own households. You will be surprised to know how many families do not invest quality time to listen to one another intently. As a leader, you must create an atmosphere—void of distractions—to listen and engage those you lead. Be present, but also carry a presence in the lives of the people you lead and serve.

it is not enough just to be present; you must establish a presence.

Never underestimate your presence. One night, during our daily talks, my wife reminded me of this. She said, "Brian, your presence here in the home makes a difference; never forget that. We feel safe, secure, loved, and at peace when you are here." It was not just because I was there, but it was the spirit that I walked in. Remember, it is not enough just to be present; you must establish a presence. Being present speaks to an individual in the context of physical proximity. However, an established presence speaks of the weight and influence that a person's spirit carries that is perceived by others. If you establish a strong presence, your presence will remain even when you are absent. Moses understood this when he was speaking with

God about the direction and destiny of the children of Israel. God had enough of Israel's stubbornness and told Moses that He would instead send His angel to go before them to lead them. He also said that the angel would also drive out their enemies. However, His presence will not be among the people unless He may destroy them for their stubbornness and unbelief. When the people heard this, they mourned. Moses pleaded with God and reminded God that Israel was His people whom He led out of Egypt. He told God that if His presence did not go with them into the land of promise, he did not want to go. It was not enough for Moses to be led by an angel of God and told the way to go. Moses craved God's presence to accompany Him. Moses felt safe, secure, loved, peaceful, and confident as a leader under the weight of God's presence. God's glory carried grace, favor, goodness, mercy, and so much more. More than anything else, the desire for God's presence should be the heartbeat of every leader. You want God's presence to be in your household, ministry, job, business, community, and nation. Please be present and establish a presence in the lives of those you are assigned to. People should be able to experience God and see the heart of God through their lives. We have too many community leaders who are distant. Too many fathers and mothers who are distant. Too many husbands and wives who are distant. Too many managers and leaders who are distant. Remember, you are an image bearer, and made in His likeness. You carry the presence of God inside of you. Your mission is to reveal God's glory in every place or person He has assigned you to. When you fail to manifest God's presence in the lives of those assigned to you, it leaves room for disorder and chaos to establish itself in you. As a leader, lacking the established presence of God leaves the people under you vulnerable without walls. A distant and aloof leader can cause those around them to believe that they do not care. People lose hope when they perceive that you do not care about them. Be courageous enough to engage the people you are called to lead. Even if you do not understand them fully, do not be afraid to try. Ask questions and solicit feedback. Inquire about their welfare and take the time to pray for them. Most importantly, engage God in prayer and pursue the presence of God. An effective leader is a compassionate leader who is motivated to inquire about the welfare of those around them. You will be surprised at what you learn and do not know about those you are called to lead and love. Leaders, take the time to listen to your colleagues, congregation, and community. Listening and knowing the state of the people is imperative to not only being a great leader but essential to providing solutions that will help you accomplish the work God has assigned to you.

One of the greatest kings and military generals in the Bible was David. He was not only a man after God's own heart but a man who believed in inquiring of God. Often, we do not acknowledge God in our course of action. We execute first, then attach God's name to it and expect Him to bless it without inquiring. If you are not open to the leading of the spirit of God and executing His purpose, then you are unfit to lead others because you are not led. King David inquired of the Lord, and God answered him. God revealed to the king winning strategic battle plans that resulted in major victories for the nation He was called to lead. Wouldn't it be amazing to have God give you winning strategic plans for the battles and conflicts you face in your life? You cannot just be strong enough to step up and lead, but you must be humble enough to kneel and seek God's direction in prayer.

LEADERSHIP PRINCIPLE 3:
Know the State of the People

Jesus was moved with compassion in His earthly ministry. He was in tune with His disciples and the people he ministered to. You, as a godly leader, must imitate Jesus in this way. Engage, listen, learn, love, and lead. The Bible says that Jesus was touched by the feelings of our infirmities. He knew that we were in a weak state and knew the temptations that we faced. He knew our state, not just because He was God. He knew because He was present with us. Jesus was sent to the world to redeem us from the power and penalty of sin. He lived among us and witnessed everything we faced. He also established a presence by revealing the nature and power of God on earth. He showed us the heart of the Father and how we should treat one another. Also, He established such a presence in every believer through the Holy Spirit. With His spirit, go and establish a presence in your assigned area of dominion.

Scriptures references to read:

- **Galatians 6:2-5,**
- **Hebrews 4:14,**
- **2 Corinthians: 15-17,**
- **Romans 5:6-11,**
- **Ephesians 5:1-2**

Introspection Moment

1) What type of leader am I? Place a circle around the answer.

   a) Distant & Passive b) Observant & Present c) Controlling & Inconsiderate

2) What state of mind are I and the people I am called to lead?
3) Am I truly pursuing the presence of God in my life and leadership?
4) What actionable steps can I take to create more of a presence in the lives of the people I am called to lead?

THE POSTURE OF LEADERSHIP

*"And it came to pass, when I heard these words, that
I sat down and wept, and mourned certain days, and
fasted, and prayed before the God of heaven"*

(NEHEMIAH 1:4 KJV)

Consistently seeking the face and favor of God on behalf of those you are called to lead is a vital part of leadership. Nehemiah inquired about the people's welfare and intervened by petitioning God for favor through prayer and fasting. Nehemiah first heard of the news of his people and the city walls having been destroyed in the month of Chisleu, which is the months of November-December. He did not get a chance to make his request known to the king until 4-5 months later in Nisan. As a leader, you may carry people's burdens for an appointed time until God provides a breakthrough. This is often hard because everything in you wants to fix the problem and save the day immediately. However, we all know they are just some things out of our control, and we cannot fix them ourselves. We need God to intervene and turn things around. As a leader, you must always remain diligent and steadfast in prayer as you petition the King of Kings.

God is looking for someone to stand in the gap and entreat His favor. You have been silent for too long. Do not allow outside voices to silence your faith. It is time to open your mouth and intervene on behalf of your family, neighborhood, job, and nation. Many of you are accustomed to waiting for someone else to come along and solve problems. What if I told you God has raised you to be a vessel through which solutions are revealed? An effective leader knows how to initiate and engage. This is first accomplished through the power of fasting and praying to God. In prayer, ask God for His grace, mercy, and favor in times of need. Many of us are familiar with the process of applying to a lender for a mortgage or a credit card. Depending on how you measure up to that financial institution's qualifications and criteria determine an approval to extend credit. When God favors you, it does not depend on you or your works because, truthfully, no one measures up to God's qualifications or criteria. That is why it is important to believe in the Lord Jesus Christ. You are qualified and approved through Christ in the sight of God. When God favors you, it is based on His good pleasure and will. I challenge you to petition God the Father—the provider of everything we need.

Nehemiah understood how to seek God's face and petition God. After hearing the distress of His people and how they were in fear, shame, guilt, hopelessness, and pain. Nehemiah mourned for days for his people. It is okay to feel or show deep sorrow when the people you love around you are hurting. However, be careful not to stay there in those feelings. Notice the Bible said that he mourned for certain days. That phrase, "certain days," means it was a mourning process or series of phases that progressed. There may have been some days when Nehemiah was just feeling so much regret. Then, the feeling of regret evolved into anger or frustration. Nevertheless, the period of mourning was progressive in nature, and it had to run its course.

Many of us are still grieving or mourning and functioning from a place of regret. It could have resulted from the loss of a loved one. Or it could have resulted from a divorce or relationship you have invested all of yourself into. Suddenly, it all ends in heartache. It could have been the loss of a career or business opportunity. It could have been simply an act of disobedience to the revealed will of God for your life, and now you are living with the consequences of your actions. We all have experienced some disappointment or failure that led us to a place of deep regret. Remember, disappointment is just an emotional response to a failed expectation. As a leader, resist the temptation of being led by your emotions. Give place to the spirit of truth and do the will of God. You cannot afford to stay here in this place of regret. You must command your soul to move forward through prayer. Take your regret to God and turn that regret into repentance. Yes, change your mind set about what you regret and accept the mindset of Christ. Obtain God's divine perspective about your situation through prayer and the Word of God. Once you repent and accept what God has said, endeavor to obey it. Align yourself in agreement with His word. You will then find your emotions and attitude submitting and conforming to the will of God. You will find yourself breaking free from those emotions while pressing into victory. Again, I say do not allow your emotions to lead you, but lead your emotions through prayer and the word of God.

As a leader, the Word of God must be the authority and tutor to guide your actions. Nehemiah understood that He served a covenant-keeping God who extended mercy to those who love Him and obey His commands. He knew this was not the end and that God would never forsake His people. Nehemiah was convinced that God was still their God and that they were His chosen people. He reminded himself that His God was a faithful, merciful, and loving God. A God who hears him when he calls. He recalled that if he and his people were to turn to God and obey, God would bring them back to the place He had chosen. A place where God's name is glorified.

Take this time to reflect on where you are and what it is called. Is it a place of regret, confusion, or hopelessness? Ask yourself if you are in the place God has chosen and called you to. Is His name being glorified in this place where you are now? If the answer is no, then quickly decide to move now. Move to where God has prepared and called you to.

Nehemiah acknowledges and confesses the wrongs he and his people have committed against God. I am highlighting this point because before we can rebuild and restore what has been torn down, we must start with reconciliation with God. We often leave out the importance of repentance. Changing our minds about our wrongs and agreeing with His truth is a prerequisite to leadership. There must be a sense of sincere, godly sorrow for what we have done. We must not make excuses and blame others. We must first acknowledge our wrongs, take responsibility, and be accountable to God for our wrongs. Next, we must be accountable to the people we are called to lead.

The great news is that our God is so rich in mercy He does not hold grudges or stay angry forever. He promises to forgive us for our sins and to cleanse us of all unrighteousness. Therefore, since we have the Lord Jesus Christ as our advocate and always making intercession for us, we can be confident that we have peace with God. Following that same model of Christ, we, as leaders, know that Jesus Christ is making intercession for us; we must intercede on behalf of the people we are called to lead as well. The people you are called to lead may not know you are praying for them. They may not even be grateful or appreciative that you take the time to pray; do not let this stop you. This is what you were called to do. You must have a heart for the people and a desire to fear God's name primarily. The first thing you will learn throughout this book is we cannot control the responses of others, but we can control our responses. The key to victory is not responding in a worldly way but letting your responses be consistent with the new nature you have through Jesus Christ.

LEADERSHIP PRINCIPLE 4:
Maintain Your Spiritual Posture

The term posture speaks to the body's positioning, which determines your balance, stability, and ability to react. When I refer to maintaining your spiritual posture. I am referring to maintaining a spiritual position so that you remain balanced, stable, and in alignment with the heart of God. When your spirit and heart are in the right posture, you can draw near to Him and receive God's presence as well. The Lord draws near to those that are broken before him. Nehemiah understood this principle when he was fasting and mourning for his people. As a leader, you want to always seek God's favor on behalf of those you lead. You must be an intercessor standing in the gap for others. A leader who is insensitive to the pains of others—is, without doubt—insensitive to the heart of God. Not only should the hurts of others grieve you, but the sins of others should also grieve you. It should always be your desire to see others restored to God and His righteousness. Prayer keeps your heart sensitive to the leading of the spirit of God. This posture will be essential when it comes to restoring and leading others.

Scriptures references to read:

- **Psalm 34:18,**
- **Ephesians 6:18,**
- **James 4:8,**
- **James 5:16,**
- **1 Timothy 2:1,**
- **Romans 8:26,**
- **Hebrews 7:25**

Introspection Moment

1) Am I spiritually aligned and responsive to the heart of God? If not, what is preventing me from doing so?
2) Do I have areas in my life where I am harboring regret and disappointment? If so, what happened to drive me to this place of regret and disappointment?

3) Am I guilty of blaming others for my shortcomings, or do I take responsibility for my decisions?
4) What actionable steps do I need to make to move from getting aligned with God's will for my life?

VEILING THE VISION

"And I arose in the night, I and some few men with; neither told I any man what my God had put in my heart to do at Jerusalem"
(NEHEMIAH 2:12 KJV)

When God puts a vision in your heart, you cannot tell everyone. I have often seen people share their dreams, ideas, and successes with others. Only to have negativity, opinions, and doubt of others, drown them in fear. Fear will distort the vision. Do not reveal the plans until an appointed time. It can be tempting because we are so excited or overwhelmed at the possibilities of launching or doing something great. Remember, God showed it to you; only you can see it clearly through faith. Others, with their natural eyes, will not always see the vision God has shown you and may discourage you. Joseph had to learn this the hard way. In Genesis 37:5-11, Joseph dreamed and told it to his brethren, and they hated him yet the more. Joseph then dreams again, and he tells his brethren again. This time, he goes into detail about the dream. Genesis 37:7 says, "For, behold, we were binding sheaves in the field, and lo, my sheaf arose, and also stood upright; and behold, your sheaves stood round about, and made obeisance to my sheaf." Immediately, his brothers understood and interpreted the meaning of the dream. And his brother said to him will you really rule over us? And they hated him yet more for his dreams and words.

"Let us pay close attention to why they hated Joseph even more. They hated Joseph for his vision and for his words. Some people will hate you because of the vision and the word God has given you. Vision and words are a powerful combination. Vision speaks to a divine insight revealed by heaven of a future reality. Your words are a declaration and statement of faith that you believe what God has revealed to you as truth. When you believe, you speak. When you speak, there is accountability. The problem with this is if you speak before time, you are accountable for something that is not ordained to run until an appointed time. We must be good stewards of the vision and secrets God shares with us. We must walk in wisdom and discernment when heaven reveals a matter to us. This is why sharing your vision with others is not always wise until an appointed time. Joseph dreams another dream and tells his father and brothers. His father rebukes him openly, and his brothers envy Joseph from that day forward. Envy means to bear a grudge or resentment towards someone due to desiring what another person has, without regard for the rights of others. Today, the spirit of envy runs rampant throughout corporations, ministries, and families. Some are people tormented by the success of others. They want your successes or accomplishments for themselves. People with this spirit will take delight in attacking, hoping to diminish and rob you of what you have. Joseph's brothers resented him and wanted his vision for themselves.

Warning to every leader: do not fall into this trap of jealousy or envy. Keep your eyes on the vision and work God has given you. Do not get caught up in what other visionaries are doing and their successes. Do not allow the spirit of competitiveness to blind you to what God wants to accomplish through you. God has given you unique gifts, skills, talents, work, and vision. Apostle Paul understood this concept. In Romans 15:20, he says, "Yea, so have I strived to preach the gospel, not where Christ was named, lest I should build upon another man's foundation." As a leader, you are a builder and visionary. You do not want to give the enemy room to sabotage or discourage your plans. Move in silence and in faith. This is not the time to post it on social media. This is not the time to put in a group chat what God told you. **I repeat, move in silence**. They will come a time when you can let people know the work God has proposed for you to do. There will also be people who fear God and can offer godly counsel and support. Allow God to direct your next course of action. Take the time to inspect thoroughly and discern the damage and risks involved. Nehemiah took only a few men with him to Jerusalem in the cover of nightfall. Nighttime was not a peak busy hour, and Nehemiah knew he would not be noticed. He used that time of privacy to be observant and discern the problem. Be diligent and intentional in discovering solutions to problems. Many out here call themselves realists because they believe they have all the facts in the natural world. However, for those who walk with God by faith, what we see in the spirit is a reality. Jesus says in Luke 14:28, "For which of you intending to build a tower, sitteth not down first, and counteth the cost, whether he have sufficient to finish it." Before you begin work, count the cost. Assess the risk and what damage has been done so you know what is lacking. Truthfully, this is where you will be fruitful. Learn to discern what is lacking and provide what is needed. Whatever is lacking, God can supply, so do not let that stop you. Now that you know what you need, it is time to rally up the most valuable resources, which are people.

"Then answered I them, said unto them, The God of heaven, he will prosper us; therefore, we his servants will arise and build: but ye have no portion nor right, nor memorial, in Jerusalem"
(NEHEMIAH 2:20 KJV)

Not everybody can share in helping with this divine project. Some people want to have their hands on something but do not genuinely believe in the vision or purpose. These types of people do not wish to see the vision or plans truly succeed, but they want to lay claims to it. They are only in it for the benefits and glory. They are the people who will quickly remind you that they are the reason for your success. Only God will get the glory on this. Self-interest seekers will have to be omitted from this splendid work. Do not waste your time with these people. God has assigned people to assist you in the work. You will be able to identify them because they will not be self-seeking. Encourage the people that God is on our side, and He will give them success. Remember, God will allow you to find favor and provide every resource you need. Now that you have the favor of God and all of heaven backing you up. It is time to work. Let us get started.

LEADERSHIP PRINCIPLE 5:
Veil the Vision

John 7 lets us know that during the time of the feasts of tabernacles. Jesus finds himself being sought after by the Jews because they want to kill Him. Jesus' brothers told Him to leave Galilee and go to Judaea so that even His disciples may see the works that He does. They told Jesus that no man does anything in secret or privately when you seek to be known openly. They wanted Jesus to show himself to the world. You may be thinking the same thing. It is time to show myself to the world because I want the world to know me and what I have to offer. However, the Bible lets us in on the motives of the brothers of Jesus. They said this because they never believed in Jesus. You may have family members, friends, and coworkers who may encourage you in your face, but inwardly, do not believe in the vision or work God has given you. They are blinded by familiarity. When people are familiar with you, it is hard to see what God has destined you to be and do. His family held a perspective of Jesus as their big brother, Jesus, the carpenter, but not as Jesus, the Son of God, the savior and king.

Do not be discouraged by what it looks like now. God has chosen you to be a repairer of the breach. The same people God is calling you to help will at first be the same people who criticize you, insult you, and take you as a joke. Jesus responds to His brothers by saying, "My time has not yet come." As a leader, you must understand the principle of God's timing. In Greek, it is called Kairos, which speaks of God's appointed time. You must not let the opinions of others pressure you to reveal or do something out of time. Your vision or work is like a woman who conceived of a baby God has given. You are to nourish, cherish, and carry the baby until full term. If a baby is born prematurely, the likelihood of that baby's survival drastically declines. Your baby may be a relationship, business, ministry, or whatever God has given you. Allow God to lead you into His divine timing. Take the time to count the cost, assess the risks, do your research, and do due diligence. Bring only a few with you, but do not fully reveal what God has put in your heart to do until an appointed time. Some people cannot handle the weight of the vision all at once. You may have to uncover it in phases and let it run its course. However, Jesus was the prophesied messiah. Israel did not fully know what God's entire plan was. As Jesus' disciples followed Him, He did not tell them that He would go to the cross until an appointed time. Although Jesus resurrected from the dead, ascended into heaven, and commissioned His disciples to go and preach the good news. They did not know that God would include the Gentiles in the plan of salvation. God's plan is always unfolding, as should your God-ordained vision.

Scripture references to read:

- **Habakkuk 2: 2-3,**
- **Ephesians 1:3-14,**
- **John 7**

Introspection Moment

1) What are some risks associated with beginning this work in my heart?
2) What are some risks associated with not beginning this work that I have in my heart to do?
3) Am I willing to pay the cost to see this vision come to pass?
4) What actionable steps must I take to ensure I can complete this project?

03

DO NOT TAKE IT PERSONAL

*"But it so happened, when Sanballat heard that
we were rebuilding the wall, that he was furious
and very indignant and mocked the Jews"*

(NEHEMIAH 4:1 KJV)

To mock means to ridicule, insult, or imitate as to make fun. Any time you decide to take God seriously and be about your Father's business, the enemy will be there to make you look like a fool. Every leader will experience insults at one point or another. Know that mocking is rooted in anger. The enemy is mad that you are courageous enough to work and seeks to discourage you. He will always try to make you feel less than. He wants you to be in a state of defeat and hopelessness. If the enemy can convince you that you are wasting your time, then he knows you will never answer the call to lead. His major goal is to get you to stop the work before you even start. Nehemiah encountered this when his enemies mocked him and the Jews for attempting to rebuild the city walls of their homeland in Jerusalem. His enemy despised him and looked at the Jews as weak people. However, Nehemiah responded by praying to God in faith and that the Lord would rise in their defense. He realized that rebuilding the wall was a symbol of restoration for his people and a display of the Lord Almighty's strength and protection. When you find yourself being insulted by others who say you are too weak, not intelligent enough, not popular enough, not attractive enough, or not gifted enough to accomplish what God has given you. Do not take it personally or wear their insults as your garments. Allow God to reaffirm who He is to you by seeking His face. Your perspective changes when you are assured of who God is in your life. When your perspective changes, then the enemies' insults will not have the power to control how you respond. I have discovered that the enemy is not insulting or mocking you, but he is insulting the God we serve. David, the young shepherd boy anointed by God, would later become king of Israel. Before he reached the palace, he had to face many battles and a giant named Goliath.

In 1 Samuel 17:43 KJV, "The Philistine said unto David, Am I a dog, that thou comest to me with staves?" And the Philistine cursed David by his gods. Goliath considered David to be nothing more than just a weak little boy of no importance. He believed that his opponent was not even worthy of stepping on the battlefield against him. Goliath was a giant and a champion amongst his people in Gath. The Philistines were a warlike people and engaged in heavy conflict with Israel. The Philistines did not respect the people of Israel nor took the God of Israel seriously. Goliath proceeds to curse David by his gods. However, David was confident that God could deliver him and the army of Israel. He realized that he was in covenant with God and that his enemies were the Lord's enemies. In 1 Samuel 17:26, David says, "For who is this uncircumcised Philistine that he should defy the armies of the living God"? David understood the power and principle of a covenant relationship. In ancient times, the people would "cut" covenants as a sign. The covenant was a binding agreement between two parties. People who were in covenant together were a united force. Their allies were your allies, and your enemies were now their enemies. To establish a covenant, one of the rituals conducted was a cutting of the flesh. Both parties would cut their wrist and clasp their arms together. It was a blood covenant that left a mark on each other. After the clasping of arms together, they would take the dirt off the ground and rub it over their flesh where the cut was. This would then leave a mark on their wrist. Anyone who saw this mark knew you were not alone and had allies. When God established His covenant with Abraham and his descendants, He required every male to be circumcised. This circumcision was a cutting of the foreskin to serve as a sign of the covenant between God and His people. God and His people were now considered united. Israel's enemies were now God's enemies. When David asked who is this uncircumcised Philistine. David was saying who is this man who is not in covenant with the one true God. David knew that he was not alone and that God was fighting for him. David came at the adversary in the name of the Lord of Hosts and defeated the giant. He defeated the giant with only a sling and a stone. He did not have the same armor as the soldiers of Israel. David did not have the same weapons that were standard in military combat. These items were uncomfortable and foreign to young David. However, he had the courage to face the enemy while everyone else was paralyzed with fear. Where did David get that courage? 1 Samuel 17:37 tells us that David reminded King Saul that the Lord had delivered him many times before. The Lord delivered him from the paw of the lion and bear. The same God would deliver him from the hand of Goliath. You may not have gone to the same Ivy League school or have degrees on the wall. You may not be the best communicator or best dressed. The question is not what you have but who you have with you. When you have God on your side, and you stand in the name of the Lord. You are standing in His authority and power. You have what you need to face every giant in your life. There will be no enemy or man who can stop you with God on your side.

Therefore, as a leader, you must understand this principle of a covenant relationship with God. You and God are a united force. All of heaven is backing you up; you are not alone. I know the opposition that you are facing may seem like a giant. However, I charge you to stand and face your giants. When you stand and resist the enemy and submit to God by forgetting your pride, reputation, title, or inadequacies. God will rise and show Himself strong on your behalf. This battle is bigger than you, and this work is not about you. It is about God and the people you are called to lead. The Lord will defend and protect His name. He will honor His word and covenant with His covenant people. The goal of victory is that all the earth may know there is still a God in Israel, Dallas, Chicago, New Orleans, and Charlotte (Put your city, state, nation, and household in there). The second goal of victory is that those around you may know that the Lord saves, not with human strength. Do not be tempted to adopt the weapons and strategies of the world. Those weapons and ways will not grant you success against the giants you will face, for this battle is the Lord's. The Lord knows how to defend His name. He shall not be mocked. Continue to sow good seeds of righteousness and maintain a mind to work. Know that God is fighting for you.

LEADERSHIP PRINCIPLE 6:
Do Not Take It Personal

Do not take it personally, but take it to God in prayer. Every challenge, every threat that is taunting and ridiculing you. Spread it before the Lord, knowing that He hears you. Watch God arise and defend His great name! Remember, the enemy is trying to make you look at you. Keep your eyes focused on Jesus. Our identity is in Him, and we lack nothing. Draw strength from the principles of covenant that you have discovered. Your enemies are God's enemies. Know that with God, you have all you need to defeat the opposition you are facing. You are not alone.

Scripture references to read:

- **2 Kings 19:1-7,**
- **1 Samuel 8: 7,**
- **Genesis 12:2-3,**
- **Romans 4:11,**
- **Deuteronomy 7:9,**
- **Romans 8:31-37**

Introspection Moment

1) What insults have I taken personally and allowed to weaken me?
2) How has the principle of covenant changed my perspective?
3) Are there giants in my life that I find intimidating?
4) What actionable steps do I need to take to confront these giants?

Key Terms

Define the terms below in your own words.

A. Covenant

B. Mock

CLOSING THE GAPS

"But it came to pass, that when Sanballat, and Tobiah, and the Arabians, and the Ammonites, and the Ashdodites, heard that the walls of Jerusalem were made up, and that the breaches began to be stopped, then they were very wroth."

(NEHEMIAH 4:7 KJV)

When your adversaries realize you will not be a coward. When they realize that making fun of or insulting you will not stop your progress. They become even more angry and frustrated. That is why you do not have to do much talking and promoting what you are doing. Allow the work to do the speaking for you. Demonstration is the best answer for those who doubt and try to hinder your work. Jesus told the unbelieving people in John 10:37-38, "If I do not the works of my Father, believe me not. But if I do, though ye believe not me, believe the works; that ye may know, and believe that the Father is in me, and I in him." Let the work speak on your behalf. You do not have to prove who you are to people; let the work of God testify to who sent you.

We talked about fighting against opposition from the outside. What do you do when the opposition is coming from within yourself? As leaders, we are quick to engage in other people's issues and problems. We have a word, strategy, counsel, encouragement, and faith to believe for everyone else. However, when the time comes for us to confront, encourage, strategize, counsel, and have faith concerning our problems, we coward away. The problem is not always the enemy, but sometimes it is just the inner me. As leaders, we must be courageous enough to confront and close the gaps in these areas in our lives. If not, then these vulnerable areas will be exploited by our foe. The enemy uses those weak and vulnerable inner battles that are in the form of doubt, fear, unforgiveness, miscommunication, and unprofitable conversations. He also exploits selfish ambition, greed, pride, lust, and distractions as an opportunity to destroy you. That is why it is pivotal for you to identify the weak and vulnerable areas and strengthen them. It is time to cover the areas the Holy Spirit has shown you that may expose you to the enemy. It starts by allowing the Holy Spirit to heal and renew those broken parts of us. The Holy Spirit will expose and strengthen those weak, vulnerable areas we have left hidden. He will build a solid foundation through Jesus Christ from which we can have authentic confidence.

When your enemy sees that he cannot deter or discourage you, he will go after those closest to you. It may be with a spouse who finds a reason to disagree with you and picks arguments. It may be a wayward child who allows outside influences to diminish the values and morals you have instilled in them. There may even be coworkers who refuse to cooperate with you. It feels like they are sabotaging all your efforts. It may be a church member who does not want to come in alignment, causing further confusion within the body. I know you are frustrated right now because the very ones you love are causing the most hurt. They may not realize how much you are fighting for them and that you want the best for them. Before you are tempted to walk out, lash out, or create further opposition, remember that they are not the enemy. Say it with me; they are not the enemy. The enemy is not your spouse, your kids, that team member, that congregation member, or your colleague. The enemy is Satan and all his evil workers. The enemy wants to find gaps so he can further divide, sabotage, weaken, destroy, and cause the work of the Lord to cease.

Think back on what we discovered about the spirit of Amalek. The Amalekites were Israel's first enemy they encountered when God delivered them from Egypt. These are the same people who attacked Israel from behind. However, Israel crossed over into a place of victory, freedom, and everlasting covenant with God. Opposition was always near as they pressed forward to possess all God had promised them. The Amalekites were known to be crafty, manipulative, and sneaky, and they targeted the weak. When traveling in large numbers, it was common for the weak to struggle behind. To be weak means to faint or lack strength. To be vulnerable speaks to being easily influenced, attacked, and damaged. Spiritually weak people are the most prone to easy influence and damage by the enemy. The reason is that they are weak in faith and lack spiritual discernment or knowledge. These are stragglers in the faith that we must watch and cover. They are journeying along but lack the faith, discernment, and endurance to complete the journey. The Amalekites were so treacherous that they would even side with Israel's enemies just to take them down. They made alliances with Moab. They partnered with the Midianites during Gideon's time as judge. The Amalekites kept popping up throughout Israel's history to come against them repeatedly, even during King Saul's reign as King of Israel.

In 1 Samuel 15:3, God had instructed King Saul to eradicate all the Amalekites and everything that belonged to them. However, the king spared Agag, who was king of the Amalekites. He also saved the best of the livestock and everything else that had value. King Saul did an incomplete job and did not fully obey the word of the Lord. Let me interject right here and warn you. To be a leader, you must know that good intentions are no longer good enough. God is looking for leaders who will totally obey and submit to Him. Leaders who take responsibility with no excuses. Finding fault and blaming others will have to be depleted from our mindset. If you reject God's word and instruction, God will reject you as His chosen leader. When God rejects you, He tears away what He has given you.

King Saul learned this the hard way. God had His prophet Samuel anoint another who would be King of Israel. You may know him as King David. In 1 Samuel 30, we see that the Amalekites had invaded the Southwest side of Judah. They burned the city down with fire and took captive all who were there. This included the wives, sons, and daughters of King David and his military men. Also, some citizens of that city were taken captive. What do you do when your past keeps showing up in your present to rob you of your future? King David had just come off a successful military campaign, only to arrive home to find those he swore to defend taken hostage by enemy forces. An enemy that was not supposed to be there in the first place. The Amalekites were the same people that God instructed King Saul to eradicate. However, because of the disobedience of King Saul, Israel suffered a loss. There are people or things that you are still battling against that are hindering and destroying your progress. Not only is it hindering your progress, but currently, it is hindering your family's progress. You neglected to confront those issues you were having when you were single. Currently, it is surfacing up into your marriage. You refuse to face the trauma that happened to you as a child. Currently, it is invading your children's life. Currently, everything attached to you seems to be under attack because you pacified an enemy that God commanded you to eradicate long ago. It is holding your business back from reaching its full potential. It is diminishing your ministry and ability to give God glory. All because you did not put to death the enemies of your soulish past, it is here robbing you of your spiritual destiny. As a leader, you will have to pursue and conquer these enemies of your past. Do not try to hide and conceal it any longer. God is with you, and you shall recover all without fail.

LEADERSHIP PRINCIPLE 7:
Close the Gaps

Evaluate your life first. Identify what is left exposed and confront it. Half the battle is acknowledging that you have gaps. Now, repair the breaches with a biblical solution. Leaders, do not allow discord or disunity to linger within your lives or among the people you lead. Set a watch over the weak and vulnerable areas. Bring your family/team together and build an agreement. Put a stop to idle talk amongst your team or family. Idle words lead to confusion and cause more distractions. Clear the air by promoting an atmosphere of encouragement, respect, and productivity towards goals. Confront these areas by exposing them to the truth of God's word. Another strategy for closing gaps is by educating and strengthening yourself and your team. Inform them exactly how the enemy was able or could come in and exploit these areas if not addressed. Let them know that everyone is vital and responsible for keeping watch and getting the work done. There must not be any weak links or breaches within your team. Get everyone up to speed by providing adequate training and coaching in the weak areas. When the people unite and have a mind to work, restoration can occur.

Scripture references to read:

- **Isaiah 62:6,**
- **Ezekiel 3:17,**
- **Habakkuk 2:1,**
- **Nehemiah 4:9.**

Introspection Moment

1) What doors have I left open that may be at risk of hindering my present and future?
2) Is there a disconnect in my fellowship with God? If so, what is causing this disconnect?
3) What actionable steps do I need to take to close the gaps in my life and with those I lead?

CONQUERING CONSPIRACY

"And conspired all of them together to come and to
fight against Jerusalem, and to hinder it"

(NEHEMIAH 4:8 KJV)

ehemiah's adversaries planned to attack the workers without them knowing or seeing until it was too late. They noticed and heard the complaints of the people of Judah. The citizens of Judah were complaining that the workers were getting tired and that there was still much debris from the demolition that needed to be moved. The workers believed that the wall could not be rebuilt. As they were complaining, the enemy was conspiring. The Jews who lived near the enemy came and told Nehemiah that the enemy was planning to attack from all directions. Their enemies were planning to come upon them unexpectedly to kill them and cause the work to cease. Yes, you have a real enemy conspiring against you with hopes of catching you off guard and causing the work of God to stop.

To conspire means to plan together secretly, to work together for any purpose or effect, to plot and scheme. The enemy will join, make alliances to become stronger, and devise schemes to hinder the work. His goal is to throw the work into confusion. Again, the root of this opposition is anger. The enemy aims to intrude by taking advantage of footholds open to him. That is why it is imperative that, as their leader, you must close the gaps. You cannot afford any breaches. Once the enemy gains a foothold, he will have a competitive advantage. He will have grounds to cause confusion and chaos because you left an opening for him. If the enemy cannot discourage you, then he will try to attack those closest to you. In Genesis, we can see an example of this in the Garden of Eden. Remember, we discussed in Chapter 1 that you were made in God's image and likeness. He has commanded us to subdue, which means to conquer and bring under control. We also discovered that subduing involves preventing something from existing or developing. The enemy knew he could not get to Adam because he was on watch. Since Satan could not get to Adam, he decided to go after the one who was closest to him. That is when Satan disguised as a snake and approached Eve. He was able to deceive Eve and get to Adam, which caused sin to enter the world. Adam was not deceived, but Eve was. If Adam had not partaken of the fruit, then he would have been separated from his wife. This is a hard test for any man and leader to face. However, every leader will face this test of loyalty at some point in their life. The question is, who will you be more loyal to, God or others? For Adam, God brought the best thing that ever happened to him into his life in the person of Eve. The thought of being separated from Eve may have been too much for Adam to manage. Nevertheless, that was the day man took the greatest fall in history. Leaders, please make God your priority. Do not allow your spouse, kids, friends, ministry, or anything to become an idol. The day you do is the day you will fall greatly. As leaders, we must keep watch over everything attached to us. Keep watch over your household, finances, team morale, and productivity. Everyone must be of one accord. Do not be afraid of the enemy. You know his attacks, so you know how to counter them. One of the enemies' major attacks against you may come in the form of confusion. Confusion causes division and distractions and weakens your team. If the enemy succeeds in causing division within your team, then he will hinder the work.

One of the ways the enemy sow's confusion is by building strongholds in the minds of the people you lead. A stronghold is where a specific cause or belief is strongly defended and upheld. Strongholds are built upon the foundation and seeds of lies you have accepted as truth. These seeds can go as far back as your childhood. It amazes me how so many of us normalize the traumatic abuse we have experienced in our lives since childhood. Just because it has always been done does not mean it was right. People have been living in dysfunction for so long that they feel uncomfortable in an atmosphere of peace, joy, truth, and righteousness. The lies that the enemy has embedded in your memory and mind must be confronted. This is achieved through uprooting the lie. Confront that lie and demolish it by the word and spirit of God. Many of us are self-sabotaging and hindering the work of God in our lives because we never confronted the lie. Many of our relationships, businesses, and spiritual growth never reach their full potential because of strongholds. As a leader, you must be willing to confront your past to have victory in your present and future. If you have never confronted these things, it will surface during times of opposition and hurt the people you are leading.

You can always tell those who have a stronghold built up in their mind. Because the enemy has blinded their mind, they will reject what you are saying. They believed his words; therefore, they spoke of his accord. The truth of God's word will sever the lies of the enemy. God's word is powerful and alive to bring every lie into subjection. The only way to break down strongholds is by consistently speaking and praying the truth over them. Most people do not understand that this is a spiritual battle. They fight using their flesh and carnality only to give up ground every time. Set a watch by covering yourself, family, team, and coworkers in prayer night and day. Now is the time to make sure that your family, team, coworkers, and partners close the gaps. Meaning it is time to put those assigned to you on notice. They should be of one accord in purpose, spirit, and mind. When the gaps are closed, then the enemy cannot get in. Be observant and guard your lips. This is not a time to speak idle and unfruitful words. The enemy will use your communication and pervert it to cause further confusion. Have you ever spoken with someone, and they heard something different than what you just said? It ends up causing confusion, arguments, and resentment. Do not let it get to that point. Identify it, expose it, and respond accordingly. Be observant and watch what words proceed from your mouth. Cease from unprofitable conversations. Restrain from joking too much and making an idle speech. Ensure you maintain focus, transparency, and clear communication amongst those you lead.

Every member of your team, family, or group should be able to articulate the mission, goals, and values. They must know what you believe and believe in the mission as well. Everyone must remain vigilant, cover each other's backs, and remain a unified front. Anyone who is idle will be a vessel used by the enemy to hinder the work. Ensure that everyone knows their role and works towards the same goal. We have allowed the enemy to destroy our families, relationships, and visions long enough by not closing the gap. That is why we must never take off our spiritual armor. Give your team the resources, training, and tools they need and put them in position. Nehemiah displayed this leadership as he armed every person on the walls with weapons and put them in position as the work continued. He encouraged and reminded them not to be afraid. He reinforced the essence for which they were fighting. He encouraged them to fight for their brothers, sons, daughters, wives, and houses. Remember, the Lord is great, and He is fighting for us.

Consider what your weapons of warfare are. We do not use the weapon of manipulation, which is another form of witchcraft. We do not use abusive or perverse language because blessing and cursing should not come out of the same mouth. People's beliefs, the universe, or good vibes will not ensure victory. You can burn all the sage you want, and it will not serve you well in the attacks from your enemy if you are practicing such things, especially as a follower of Jesus Christ. I plead with you to remove such things from your altar. Renounce any spells you may have cast or had cast to gain control. Repent any rituals you may have performed that are not of God. I have seen followers of Christ conform to these ungodly practices and have been entertaining demons. God is not pleased with such practices, and

He resists those who practice these things. Anything that is not done in faith in Christ Jesus is a sin. Remove and discard every instrument, such as scrolls and literature holding information about such practices. Remove and disassociate yourself from influences or influencers who practice such ungodly acts. Your weapons are not worldly weapons. The world's way of fighting is not effective and will not gain you the victory ordained by God. Carnality and evil practices will only cause further devastation.

And it came to pass, when our enemies heard that it was known unto us and God had brought their counsel to nought, that we returned all of us to the wall everyone unto his work.

NEHEMIAH 4:15 KJV

As a leader, God will not allow you to be deceived or blinded. God will not only expose the enemies' scheme, but He will frustrate the enemy's plan. The Word and Spirit of God will uncover the enemy's concealed plan, lies, and scheme. He will not leave you ignorant of Satan's devices. Our weapons of warfare are the knowledge of the Word of God. Our weapons are prayer, fasting, and praising God. We must bring every thought and thing into submission to the word of God. Yes, arrest and detain every thought and memory that has lied dormant in your mind. Examine it through the lenses of the word of God. If it does not align with the word of God, then allow the word of truth to sever every lie.

CONFRONTATION THAT CREATES CHANGE

"Now there arose a great outcry of the people and of their wives against their Jewish brothers"

(NEHEMIAH 5:1 ESV)

At some point, the people whom God has entrusted to you will have complaints. Some may complain that they are being treated unfairly by one another. A lack of respect, unity, and unrighteousness amongst the people you lead can hinder any work you put your hands to. As a leader, you are responsible for setting order by confronting all unrighteousness. Only a leader who is motivated by the fear of God and not the fear of man can accomplish this. Many people have a skewed perspective about confrontation and consider it negative to engage in. However, confrontation is not bad if executed properly. You need godly wisdom, insight, and understanding to judge rightly. If you do not have these things first, then do not initiate a confrontation. Only an obedient heart can see things clearly without distortion. Nehemiah demonstrated this during his leadership as governor. Complaints were being brought to him by the men and their wives, who had large households to feed but were experiencing a food shortage. Many of them had mortgaged their land, houses, and vineyards to their Jewish brothers to buy food because of the famine. Economic conditions were so bad that many sold their children into slavery to pay off debts. Unfortunately, their Jewish brethren profited from their pain by charging ridiculous interest rates, which they knew could never be repaid. It is equivalent to today's payday and title loan services, which enslave many borrowers with their astronomical interest rates. The Jews' conduct was a violation of God's statutes. Leviticus 25:36-37 says, "Take thou no usury of him or increase: but fear thy God; that thy brother may live with thee. Thou shalt not give him thy money upon usury, nor lend him thy victuals for increase." God was warning the people not to forget that He brought them out of the house of bondage in Egypt. He wanted them to reflect on what it was like to be taken advantage of and enslaved. Now that He has given them a land of their own, He commanded them not to take advantage or enslave their brother or sister. Nehemiah was truly angry when he heard the outcry of the people. After thoroughly considering the matter, Nehemiah brought charges against the nobles and the officials who were exploiting the people. He confronted them and told them to return everything they had taken from them. Although Nehemiah had righteous anger, he thoroughly considered each matter and executed it accordingly. He did not ignore the oppression, injustice, exploitation, or cruelty among the people he was leading. Every leader must not oppress God's people nor tolerate anyone who does so among them. The longer you allow unrighteousness to remain in your household, business, community, and churches, the more it will spread like cancer and destroy your efforts. Do not be unwilling to confront unrighteousness because you fear losing your star employee. Correct those you lead no matter how gifted or valuable they may be to your efforts. How can you expect the King of Righteousness to establish and bless the work of your hands if you allow unrighteousness to remain in the camp? I am reminded of a time when God confronted Joshua, the leader of Israel after Moses. Joshua had announced to the children of Israel that God had given the city of Jericho to them. They had the town of Jericho surrounded with all the people shut within its gates. He warned the people that everything within the gates would be devoted to the Lord for destruction. If anyone were to take anything for themselves, the Lord warned that they would bring trouble upon themselves. Not only will the individual have consequences, but such consequences will also affect the entire camp. Joshua then gives them divine instructions from God that led to the walls of Jericho falling. After the fall of Jericho, Joshua sends a few men from Jericho to Ai to go up and survey the country. The men returned and told Joshua that he should not send all the men but only a few to fight against Ai. The men reported that Ai was few, and there was no need to have all of Israel's men fight in this battle. Joshua sent three thousand men to Ai, and the men of Ai put the army of Israel to flight. What was supposed to be an easy victory became an embarrassing slaughter. The army forces of Ai killed thirty-six men while the others fled back to camp. Joshua and the elders of Israel mourned and prayed to the Lord because of this great defeat. The Lord told Joshua to get up! Why is your face on the ground? The Lord asked? The Lord revealed to Joshua that the people had sinned by stealing things that the Lord considered accursed. They took what was prohibited and hid it among their belongings within the camp. God revealed to Joshua that because of this sin, they could not stand against their enemies. Disobedience robs you of the authority, power, and insight needed to gain victory. Disobedience not only affects your own life but also those in your community. The Lord told Joshua that He was not with Israel anymore. Also, God told Joshua that if he did not confront the children of Israel, He would not be with Joshua anymore either. God was not playing with Joshua and would not allow him to pray out of this. He charged Joshua to confront the people and their unrighteousness. When Joshua discovered it was Achan who stole the silver and gold. He took him, his family, the silver, the gold, and burned them all. Let this be a lesson to every leader not to pacify unrighteousness within the camp. Call it out, confront it, and remove it. You cannot afford to bury these issues by ignoring them. Being passive in this area will rob you of God's presence and power in your life. Without God, your work will be in vain, and you will experience defeat. You will be unable to accomplish things and find yourself running from one venture to another. Hopping from one job to another. Going from one relationship to another. Going from one church to another because you refuse to confront unrighteousness. It does not have to be only unrighteousness within the camp; God may be charging you to confront things buried and hidden within your heart. These hidden things may prevent you from experiencing the presence of God in your life. The Holy Spirit may be telling you right now what these things are and where they are buried. My friend, you must dig it up, expose it through confession, and repent of it now. Allow the fire of God's spirit to consume and refine you. If you are guilty of covetousness, anger, pride, greed, and adultery, then God has instructed that you eradicate these things. If you hold on to these things, you will find yourself just like the men of Israel who went out to fight. You will find yourself running and being chased by the enemy of your soul. Things that should be an easy victory for you become challenging and unbearable. Not only will you suffer in defeat, but your whole camp will be robbed of the power and presence of God. I have witnessed many leaders' ministries, businesses, and families suffer because they refused to confront things that were not right.

In addition, people will lose respect and confidence in your leadership ability. A leader who is afraid to confront unrighteousness is weak and cowardly. In Psalms 82, God rebukes the rulers and judges of that time for not confronting unrighteousness. The rulers showed favoritism and didn't stand up for the poor or those oppressed by the wicked.

LEADERSHIP PRINCIPAL 8:
Confront All Unrighteousness

Leaders are defenders of the weak and a voice for those who do not have one. Every godly leader must execute righteousness and justice without compromise. Do not be afraid to confront all unrighteousness. Do not be tempted to coward down or compromise. You cannot change what you are not willing to confront.

Scripture references to read:

- **Psalm 82,**
- **Isaiah 1:17,**
- **Psalm 140:12,**
- **Jeremiah 22:3.**

Introspection Moment

1) In what areas of my life and assignments have I been passive?
2) Do I seek out confrontation, or do I try my best to avoid it? Why?
3) What areas in my life and assignments have I compromised?
4) What actionable steps can I take today to cease the compromises I consistently make?

> *"Even their servants Lorded it over the people. But I did not do so, because of the fear of God"*
> **(NEHEMIAH 5:15 ESV)**

Use your position and influence to benefit the work of God and those you serve. Be self-sacrificing, and do not oppress the people you serve and lead. If you are not serving, you are dictating, and that's not true leadership. Devote yourself to God and the work.

With public leadership comes authority, favor, and honor due to the office. You do not need a podium or platform to be a leader. However, there are some that God has called to lead in the public sphere. This relates to federal, state, or local government and authorities. God has given you a vehicle to exercise your leadership for His glory through a seat. Today, many refer to it as an office. An office is a public position where authority and service can be executed within an agency or government. Some leaders use their office for righteous endeavors. However, many leaders use these offices for personal gain.

Many leaders lord over people rather than serve the people. To Lord over someone means to utilize your authority to force, control, and assert your will on others without regard for their wellbeing. That is another reason many rebel against authority. When you have been abused and taken advantage of by authority, your perspective and attitude change. Distrust set in, and people began to take the law and authority into their own hands. Typically, many leaders who lead in this manner believe that they are more important than others. These people love the office lifestyle but do not love the people the office serves. In recent years, many cases have been highlighted in the media of police corruption. Many have banded together to advocate for defunding the police. Presidents and politicians have been put under investigation for misdealing's and corruption. Ministers and shepherds of God's people have been named in scandals and cases. The people you lead need to see authority demonstrated how it was designed. Under godly authority, the people are safe and at peace. The former governors before Nehemiah laid heavy burdens on the people and took advantage of them. They confiscated people's land while requiring large daily rations to be brought to them. Nehemiah refused to lead and utilize his office in this way because he feared God. Nehemiah remained diligent on the work of the wall and required no land. He sees that those under his leadership also remained focused on the work as well. He did not allow those under his leadership to exploit the people. Nehemiah demonstrated leadership for other leaders to follow.

LEADERSHIP PRINCIPLE 9:
Leverage Your Office and Influence

Like Nehemiah, use the office and leverage resources to ensure the work gets completed. Remember, God is the ultimate and supreme ruler. If you are appointed as a public leader, then lead as a minister of God for righteousness. There is a purpose for the authority God has given you. You are a vessel in the hand of God to execute judgment on those who do evil. Fear God and oppose what is not right in the sight of God. Do not oppress the people whom God has commanded to submit to your authority. For you will be held accountable for what you have done with the office entrusted to you.

Scripture references to read:

- **Romans 13:1-7,**
- **1 Peter 2:13-14,**
- **Hebrews 13:17.**

Introspection Moment

1) List some ways you can utilize your influence to support the work of God and others.
2) Am I guilty of abusing my influence and authority to take advantage of people and situations? If so, in what way?
3) Do my lifestyle and character show that I fear God? If not, then why?

04

THE ENEMY OF DISTRACTIONS

"And I sent messengers unto them, saying, I am doing a great work, so that I cannot come down: why should the work cease, whilst I leave it, and come down to you"

(NEHEMIAH 6:3 KJV)

Nehemiah's enemies heard there were no more ways to breach the wall because the gaps had been closed. As a final attempt to ensure the work was not completed, the enemy sent an invitation to meet with Nehemiah. Accepting this invitation meant that Nehemiah would have had to stop the work. He declined the invitation and kept focus on the work of God. Be cautious; the enemy will try to send you an invitation in the disguise of peace. It only attempts to get you to drop your guard and stop the work. Satan does not want peace and does not know peace. He only desires to steal, kill, and destroy you and the work of God. Let us examine the word invitation. Invitation is a written or verbal persuasion and allurement to get a person to go somewhere or to do something. Invitations from the enemy come in many forms, but their purpose is all the same. The enemy wants to persuade and lure you away from God and the work that God has given you. The enemy may use the invitation of money, fame, and power to distract you. He tried this strategy against Jesus in the wilderness. The Bible says in Luke 4 that the Spirit led Jesus into the wilderness. For about one and a half months, Jesus was tempted by the devil. Many people believe temptation or times of testing happen only instantaneously. Remember, you are dealing with an adversary who is very methodical. Do not rationalize or compromise; submit to God, and the devil will flee. Jesus shows us how to stand and resist. The devil took Jesus up to a high mountain and showed Him all the kingdoms of the world in a moment of time. The enemy believed that he had subdued all the kingdoms of the world and that he had all power and glory in his hands. He told Jesus that he would give it to Him on the condition that Jesus would worship him. However, Jesus said, "Get behind me, Satan: for it is written, you shall worship the Lord your God, and Him only shall you serve." Jesus put the distractions behind Him and kept His focus on God. As a leader, you must learn how to utilize your sword, which is the word of God. You have the Holy Spirit, who will bring all things to your remembrance. I challenge you to deposit God's written scripture daily into your life. Only then can you stand and resist the enemy. You will have the confidence and ability to say to every devil. Get you behind me, for it is written. When it is written, it carries weight and authority. The kings of the old knew that their decrees could not hold weight until they wrote them down and signed them. Even today, only what is written becomes policies, procedures, and laws. I want you to confront every devil that is trying to lead you away from God. Tell them it is written. Jesus did not focus on what He could gain from this world but on what He had with the Father. May we imitate Jesus in this way? May your relationship with God the Father be your great and exceeding reward.

In this life, there will always be distractions. People, places, and things will always strive to drag you away from God. Do not allow the cares or pleasures of this world to pull you away from your Source. Strong men like

Samson have fallen at the hands of distractions. Wise men like Solomon have fallen by the enemy of distraction. Chosen and anointed men of God like King David have fallen because of the enemy of distraction. In 1 Samuel 11, the Bible says that it happened, at the time when kings go forth to battle, that David sent Joab, his servants, and all Israel; But David stayed behind in Jerusalem. The Bible goes on to say that David arose from his bed and walked upon the roof of his house, and he saw from his roof a woman washing herself. The woman's name was Bathsheba. Bathsheba was an attractive woman who had caught the eye of the King. David inquired about her, and one of his servants said she was the married woman of one of his soldiers named Uriah. Despite this, King David sent for her, and together they had an affair. However, Bathsheba's husband, Uriah, was not rich, powerful, popular, or influential. He was a focused man who understood his purpose. Better is a poor man who is focused then a rich man who is distracted. A distracted man is a dangerous man. Secondly, do not feel obligated to accept every invitation or offer that comes your way. If an opportunity or invitation comes your way that is pulling you away from God or preventing you from accomplishing righteousness, then reject the invitation. The Bible goes on to say that Bathsheba found out she was pregnant and

A distracted man is a dangerous man.

told King David. King David knew he had to act fast, so he ordered Bathsheba's husband to return home from the battlefield. Once Uriah came to David, he asked Uriah how the battle went. After Uriah gives David an account of the activities on the battlefield, he then tells Uriah to go home to his wife, refresh himself, and take some food that he had prepared for him. Instead of going home to his wife, Uriah sleeps in front of the king's palace. He refuses the King's invitation to go home. In this, Uriah maintained his integrity. Uriah's focus was on the battlefield, where his assignment and purpose were. He could have easily accepted the invitation. After all, he has been out there on the battlefield fighting for his country. Why not take some well-deserved time off; it was harmless, right?

Remember, do not rationalize or compromise. My friend, some invitations and opportunities presented to you will appear justifiable and harmless. However, through the eyes of discernment, you will be able to uncover the deceit and craftiness of the enemy. Even if the act itself may not be evil, be cautious to avoid it. Prayerfully consider your choice and maintain your integrity. Uriah asks the King why he should go home to eat, drink, and lie down with his wife when the other men are on the battlefield. The enemy of distraction was using King David. Remember that distracted people are instruments of distraction and destruction for others, instead of King David leading on the battlefield where he belonged. He was used as an instrument of distraction and a tool for Uriah's destruction. King David ordered his captain Joab to have Uriah placed where the battle was most intense. Uriah, along with other men, died on the battlefield because of a distracted leader.

LEADERSHIP PRINCIPLE 10:
Guard Against Distraction

Today, identify any distractions in your life that may be hindering you. If it prevents you from focusing on your relationship with God, it is a distraction. Even good works can become a distraction if not properly prioritized and given boundaries. Choose the greater, which is God.

Scripture references to read:

- 1 Peter 5:8,
- Luke 4,
- Luke 10:38-42,
- Samuel 11.

Introspection Moment

1) What distractions have I allowed in my life that may be hindering me?
2) Am I guilty of placing my work and assignment above my relationship with God? If so, why?
3) Am I motivated by the idea of proving myself successful or by the intent and purpose of God?
4) If there was one distraction that I could remove immediately, what would it be?
5) What actionable step can I make today to remove that distraction?

HERE COMES THE BRIBE

"Thou shalt not wrest judgment; thou shalt not respect persons, neither take a gift: for a gift doth blind the eyes of the wise, and pervert the words of the righteous"

(DEUTERONOMY 16:19 KJV)

Do not entertain the enemy by compromising and accepting bribes or peace offerings. Remain steadfast and grounded in truth. Maintain your integrity, and do not sin against God. The enemy will try to persuade you to cut corners or make compromises regarding your faithfulness to God. Do not fall prey to this scheme. Be content in the things that God has given you from His hand. God will never leave nor abandon you, so you will always have what you need. Your adversary will try to make peace by being subtle. They will use trickery and deceit to get you to stop the work. Remember, you are doing magnificent work, so do not be available for these distractions. These distractions can come in many forms. Through people, places, or things. The enemy will deploy people in your life who may try to pull you in other directions contrary to the work God has assigned to you. They will only drain you of your strength, resources, influence, and time. Be a good steward of your time, talents, and resources. Do not allow distractions to lure these assets from you.

LEADERSHIP PRINCIPLE 11:
Do not Accept Bribes

As a godly leader, you should find it offensive to be bribed. Those who fear God despise bribes and remain true to their integrity. Since God cannot be bribed, so should His children. When you are not focused on God and the calling of God, then you open yourself to compromises that may cost your life. When you are no longer content with the things God has given you, you make room for the traps of the enemy.

Scripture references to read:

- **Deuteronomy 16:19,**
- **Exodus 23:8,**
- **Hebrews 13:5,**
- **Philippians 4:11-13,**
- **1 Samuel 8,**
- **Job 36:18.**

Introspection Moment

1) Do I truly find contentment in God or with the things I gain in this life? If not, why?
2) Have I been guilty of accepting bribes? If so, what has it cost me to accept bribes?
3) What actionable step can I take today to find contentment in the things of God?

SILENCING THE ENEMY OF SLANDER

"A good name is rather to be chosen than great riches, and loving favour is better than silver or gold"

(PROVERBS 22:1 KJV)

Nehemiah's enemy sent four more invitations, but he declined all. The opposition sent his servant the fifth time with an open letter to Nehemiah. The letter stated that it had been reported that Nehemiah and the Jews were planning a revolt against the King. This is why they are building the wall so that Nehemiah could be King of Judah. However, Nehemiah denied these claims because he knew they only wanted to strike fear. The rebels were saying to themselves that Nehemiah and the Jews shall be weakened from the work, that it be not done. The enemy deployed an attack through the power of slander. Slander is to speak an untrue statement about someone intending to damage their reputation. Since your opponents cannot destroy your work, they will not stop until they destroy your reputation. Your reputation is tied to your name. A good name is essential to every leader. A name speaks of the quality of your character and distinguishes you from others. A name also represents an individual's authority, honor, or fame. We must understand the importance of a name because if you do not, you will never understand the process of calling. To call means to give a name, publish, encounter, cause to come upon, invite, or summon. I cannot invite you if I do not know your name or location. Before I can call someone, I must know the name of the person I am calling. Isaiah 43:1 says, "But now thus saith the Lord that created thee,

O Jacob, and he that formed thee, O Israel, Fear not; for I have redeemed thee, I have called thee by thy name; thou art mine." When God said I had called thee by name, you are mine. He is saying He is already acquainted with the person He has formed. This is a hard concept for many to understand because our image and perspectives of ourselves are founded on present and past experiences. Many of us base our identity on the opinions of others. However, when God calls you, He names and transforms your identity. The enemy will always attack and attempt to slander the name God has called you. When you truly accept who God says you are and commit to the purpose of God. You will not allow yourself to be distracted by false invitations and false names the accuser will try to place over you. Let us examine what took place at the beginning—in the Garden of Eden. The enemy deceived Eve by causing her to question God's motive. Genesis 3:4-5 says, "and the serpent said unto the woman, Ye shall not surely die: for God doth know that in the day ye eat thereof, then your eyes shall be opened, and ye shall be as gods, knowing good and evil." The enemy made it seem as if God's motive for commanding Adam and Eve not to eat from the tree of the knowledge of good and evil was not pure. If the enemy would try to slander God's name, then what makes you think he will not attempt to slander the people who are called by God's name? His goal is to make you seem as if your motives are impure and false. He did it to Job when he was being tested. The adversary questioned Job's motives for serving God and brought accusations to God against Job. However, through trials and tests, Job was found not guilty and proven faithful. Look at the life of Joseph and how his name was slandered. Joseph was sold into slavery by his brothers. By God's sovereignty, Joseph was brought down to Egypt and purchased by Potiphar, who was an officer to Pharaoh. The Lord caused Joseph to prosper because the Lord was with him. Joseph found favor with Potiphar, and Potiphar made him overseer over his entire house. However, Potiphar's wife consistently attempted to seduce Joseph into sleeping with her. Each time, Joseph ran away and maintained his integrity. After being rejected by Joseph, Potiphar's wife sought revenge.

She accused Joseph of trying to have an affair with her. Joseph was then taken to prison under this false accusation and slander. Nevertheless, Joseph remained faithful and remained in his calling. Even in prison, the Lord was with Joseph and showed Joseph favor and mercy. Joseph was trusted to oversee things in prison, and God caused him to prosper. If you find yourself under the attack of slander and being falsely accused. Do not become bitter, hateful, or settle for defeat. Remain faithful to the Lord and know that He is with you. Some leaders will face this enemy of slander at some point in their journey. This is normally where falsified stories of scandal, mischief, and misconduct are brought to the public. The goal here is to strike fear or intimidate you. Your foe does not want you to complete your assignment or to establish a legacy. You will be tempted to question whether God is really with you, and you will experience doubts about the call upon your life when faced with such scrutiny. Your opposition wants to destroy your reputation, which is tied to your testimony. Do not abandon your assignment or hide in fear. He seeks to disqualify you, but remember; it is God who can cause His servant to stand. During this process, you may lose friends, associates, and contacts. However, maintain your integrity and remain faithful to God. The Lord will vindicate you and cause your righteousness to shine. One day, Pharaoh sent and called Joseph, and they brought him out of prison. They shaved him and changed his garments. Pharaoh asked Joseph to interpret his dream. When Joseph successfully interpreted the dream. Pharaoh said that there was no one as discreet and wise as Joseph. God had redeemed Joseph and caused Pharaoh to set Joseph over all the land of Egypt. By placing Joseph in position, Joseph was able to preserve the nation of Israel during a severe famine. Know that the work God has called you to lead could preserve your family, city, household, nation, or even a generation. Seek God's face for strength and clarity during this time. Those who wait upon the Lord He will renew their strength. Maintain your integrity. Daniel understood this principle of maintaining integrity. God had given Daniel an excellent spirit and caused Daniel to be promoted above people in great positions within the kingdom during the reign of King Darius of Babylon. The Bible says in Daniel 6:4, "Then the presidents and princes sought to find occasion against Daniel concerning the kingdom, but they could not find a no occasion nor fault; forasmuch as he was faithful, neither was there any error or fault found in him." When we live a faithful and integrable life, we prevent the enemy from convicting us of unrighteousness. Do not give the enemy an opportunity to have a case against you by living a compromised life. We have witnessed so many great leaders fall. Not because they were not gifted, not because they did not have vision, but because they failed to do what was right when no one was looking. We must be leaders of integrity. Whatever is done in the dark will be exposed.

THE FEARLESS LEADER

"Let us shut the doors of the temple: for they will come to slay thee; yea, in the night will they come to slay thee. And I said, should such a man as I flee"

(NEHEMIAH 6:10-11 KJV).

A s a leader, you must be strong and courageous in the face of opposition. The enemy will try to intimidate and strike fear in you. Fear is the state of withdrawing or separating oneself because of dread. It also means to put to flight, panic, or intimidate. Nehemiah's enemy hired someone to convince him to meet within the temple as a place of refuge. A false word was out that the enemy was seeking to kill him. However, Nehemiah remembered that God was on his side and there was nothing or no one to fear. I remember when the COVID-19 pandemic erupted in 2020. The world was in a state of panic and fear. Every area of society was impacted, including the church. There was a mandatory shutdown. We could not gather and fellowship corporately within church infrastructures. We could not heal or touch the sick. We became silent and faithless during this time. When the media and government began to tell lies, we had no truth to offer or answers to solve the issues. There was no compass to show the people the way to go. We lacked spiritual discernment to let the land know the mind and will of God. In a time when we were supposed to be believers, we were unbelieving. We no longer trusted God, and we doubted Him. It was a time to see what we stood on and what our foundation was made of. Fear shifted our focus.

When the enemy comes in like a raging wind, do not lose your focus. Keep your eyes on Jesus and the work He has given you to do. As a leader and warrior, it is a dishonor to turn your back to the enemy to run. Sometimes, my friend, you may have to stand alone in the face of fear. Nonetheless, you must stand. In your marriage, you may be tempted to run when things get difficult. I say to you this day, stand. You may have taken a righteous stand against a corrupt policy or against popular beliefs, and others are against you. I say to you, stand for righteousness. The true test of a leader is not only what he is willing to live for but what and for whom you are willing to die. On that night in the garden of Gethsemane, Jesus asked His disciples to sit and pray. Jesus's soul was in great sorrow because He knew the time was near that He would be betrayed and delivered into the hands of the enemy. Judas, who was one of His disciples, came with the chief priests, scribes, elders, and a crowd of people. They seized Jesus, and the Bible says all forsook him and fled.

LEADERSHIP PRINCIPLE 12:
Be A Fearless Leader

There will be things in this life that will come against you and cause you to fear. The purpose is to get you to run out of fear and forsake Jesus. As a leader, you must not forsake and abandon your God or the work God called you to. In the face of fear, Jesus pressed on to do what no one dared to do nor was qualified to do. He was crucified for our sins, and our peace with God rested on His shoulders. Jesus overcame not only fear, but He overcame death. Because of Christ, you and I are more than a conqueror. A coward is someone who lacks the courage to do or endure dangerous or unpleasant things. The Bible says in Revelation 21:7-8, "The one who conquers will inherit these things, and I will be his God, and he will be my son. But as for the cowards and unbelievers, their share is in the lake that burns with fire and Sulphur, which is the second death."

Scriptural references to read:

- **Deuteronomy 31:6,**
- **Joshua 1:9,**
- **Psalm 23:4,**
- **Psalm 46:1-3,**
- **Psalm 56,**
- **Isaiah 41:10,**
- **2 Timothy 1:7,**
- **Revelation 21:7-8.**

Introspection Moment

1) Am I leading out of fear or faith? If fear, why?
2) What steps must I take to build my confidence in Jesus Christ?

BOOK OVERVIEW

Every person born into this world will encounter various forms of adversity throughout their lifetime. However, God has chosen and positioned a few to lead others through these seasons of opposition to a place of enormous success. Chosen For Conflict is more than a book; it is a battle plan for leaders to utilize while executing the work and will of God, whether that work consists of starting a family, building a business, leading a team, serving a community, or overseeing a church. None of these things are exempt from attack and will experience conflict that requires divine strategic leadership. Twelve principles were extracted from the book of Nehemiah. Using verses from the holy scriptures and biblical illustrations, Chosen for Conflict exposes the diverse tactics deployed by the enemy to weaken and destroy your mission. Brian Dupor will teach you to assess a threat, mobilize your team, honor God, frustrate the enemy, and complete the work.

ABOUT THE AUTHOR

Brian Dupor is a husband, father, business leadership consultant, and recruiting team lead for a global transportation and logistics provider. Brian is also the founder and CEO of See & Seize Association Inc. Brian is known as a prophetic minstrel, songwriter, mentor, biblical teacher, prison volunteer leader, and pastor of a ministry founded by Brian and his wife, Princess, called We Are One Kingdom Ministries. Throughout Brian's whole life, God has allowed him to be surrounded by "complex situations" and has given him the wisdom to always find a way to bring a clear resolution. Brian now understands this was tied to his purpose by God. Now released is Brian's debut book as an author entitled Chosen for Conflict. Please subscribe and follow Brian Dupor at the following.

Links

🌐 WAOK Ministries website: waokministries.org

f Facebook page: WAOK Ministries: facebook.com/pg/waokministries

▶ YouTube channel: www.youtube.com/@waokministries3194